What's Your KICK?

The Guide To Unlocking Your Passion

By: Seanathan Polidore

Editor: Anthony G. Bell, Jr.

Artwork By: Antoine "Ghost" Mitchell

Library Of Congress Cataloging-In-Publication Data available upon request.

ISBN: 978-0-692-99177-0

Table of Contents

Acknowledgments:

I want to say a large thank you to my loving and understanding wife, Tallya. Of course, writing a book takes time and it is no easy task going through the whole book process from front to back, so she has been super supportive in my endeavors and understanding of the amount focus and discipline it would take to get this work from my mind to the pages you are about to read. I want to thank my beautiful mother, Versana Polidore. She has evolved into more than a mother to me. She is my friend and of course she is Team Sean all day so whatever I needed from her along this process she has been more than willing to bend over backwards to make sure this work is done. I want to thank Anthony Bell, Lexi Diggs, Alexis Rack, Carlos Garcia, Brian Steward, Bobby Drake, and Raymond Dockery III aka Doc for pushing me through each and every one of these chapters throughout this writing process and for allowing me to interview you for background information that went into the heart of this book. I want to take the time out to thank my Master Teacher, My mentor, My Yoda Anthony Bell. He has been like a second father to me more so than a big brother figure over the years. A lot of the principles and nuggets that I may give are a sum of our lessons over the years. The moment I get these wild ideas you are always there to guide me and support me every step of the way like a shadow over the shoulder. I want to thank Toya Dockery so much for being a trailblazer and helping me realize how much this whole book idea in the back of my mind could be a reality. Seeing the cover of your book, seeing it on Amazon, touching it, highlighting it, and sharing it with people. All of this made it very tangible for me, and it made me push harder in my writing. Thank you for ALL of your advice my sister. I cannot go on without thanking Barron Hubert Jr. for giving me the one conversation I needed to spark the thought in my mind to tackle this mountain of a task such as writing a book. I would have never had the courage or the motivation to change my entire life around to complete this work.

Lastly, I want to thank my incredible family that gives me so much Warmth, Love, Care, Support, and Belief in me. I do not take these things for granted because I cannot imagine what life would be without these "norms" in place, but then I realize that families like mine have become the exception and not the rule for a lot of people in this time that we find ourselves in. I Love you all so much and I pray that I make you proud with this work well after my time is done on this earth.I would like to dedicate this book to my Grandmother Dora Lewis. I always admired your command of words and your writing ability. You always spoke with so much power and influence for such a small person, but when you spoke everyone respected you. I know you always smile so big when I accomplish things in life. I pray this work plants the biggest smile on your face. Your first grandbaby did it! My birthday mate. I Love you Maw- Maw.

Foreword
By: Anthony Bell

As the sun rises and sets on the horizon of nothingness, one is left with a myriad of challenges, unanswered questions, accepted beliefs, and differing realities of those closest to them. With seasons of change, people come and go…family and friends change with their "perception" of you and what you can or cannot do for them in times of need. The one constant is YOU! One of the most important questions to answer is, "WHO ARE YOU?"

Do you know who you are? Do you REALLY know? Do you care, have you researched, investigated, inquired, asked questions, or have you accepted what someone else has told you OR passed down to you? When asked the question of who you are, most people will tell you their name not realizing the question remains unsatisfactorily and improperly unanswered. They merely repeat what they are referred to by association. Have you been defined by and have you defined yourself as a name, a color, a political party, a region or section of a city, a fraternity or sorority, a religious system etc., hopefully not, but if so…there is much more to YOU and your story. Most of us are not willing to delve into ourselves (personally, culturally, spiritually, individually or as a group, society, nation, and as a global concept) due to a false sense of comfort, lethargy, false reality and warped perception that one may find him or herself in, and most of all from a lack of teaching and instruction on how to. However, when that day of self-realization, self-awareness and that unquenchable insatiable "NEED TO KNOW" surfaces from deep within…EVERYTHING CHANGES. No longer are you accepting what is told, no longer are you defined by what others perceive, no longer do you accept someone else's projected "truth" onto you. Everything is questioned mathematically logical. Hence the quest of search and the inevitable "journey within" begins. When it does, replacing emotion with logic and comprehension is paramount to gaining Knowledge, Wisdom, and Under / Over standing. The process of UN-learn and RE-learn is mandatory, which has its challenges that will prove difficult due to the years of deep conditioning, deep programming from before you were born, coupled with intentional disinformation about YOU and who YOU are. The maturation process of discovery will alienate you from those you thought were friends and relatives, as "your truth" does not match with what their truth is and what they want yours to be. Stand firm on what you KNOW and not believe then maybe later those you attempt to enlighten may have the ears to hear you. Some people will not have a problem with new information as much as their problem is YOU! WORDS HAVE POWER…be careful and choose wisely the spoken word, for the "Holy Trinity" of <u>intent thoughts</u>, <u>feelings</u> and <u>spoken words</u> is everything that shapes and creates your reality whether you are aware of it or not. Poverty is a condition, but being poor is a state of mind. Conversely wealth is a condition, and being successful is also a state of mind. The condition is a result of the state of mind as there are people that ONLY want to "think" and grow rich, but do not want to do any work towards achieving their goals. Consequently, their dreams never manifest, as they remain figments of their own imagination while becoming noises of useless banter. All that was, is, and will be, involves ***work***, which entails energy: idea, plan, strategy, target audience, finance, and implementation.

Are you any different than the successful person you admire? NO! What is separating them from you? Do you KNOW what you want? Are you working towards achieving? Do you have discipline or a lack thereof? Do you move with precision, or do you randomly take steps with no direction? Do you calculate or do you round up/down? Do you live life, or simply exist from one moment to the next waiting for what life throws your way? Have you changed your routine in the last 6 months? If you want things in your life to change, you MUST CHANGE the things in your life. Change the way you think, eat and live. Is your mind programmed to be positive or negative? Mistake wise, do you repeat the same mis-take or do you learn the lesson, take heed and move on without repeating? WHO DO YOU

LISTEN TO? If you are not listening to someone that has done or is doing what you want to do, then WHY are you listening to him or her? It is the equivalent of being married and listening to someone single tell you how to stay happy and sustain a marriage! How coachable are you and how much of a sacrifice are you willing to make to get what you want? Do you play it safe, or do you take risks? Yesterday is his-story, tomorrow is a mystery, are you dealing with the here and now?

I am HONORED to serve you "Dr." Sean and am equally grateful for this opportunity to transfer this energy to your readers.

I AM THAT I AM.

Anthony Bell

Introduction

My career as a fitness trainer, psychologist, and motivational speaker has afforded me the opportunity to meet people from a wide range of ages, races and socioeconomic backgrounds from across the country. The thousands of hours that I have logged in commercial gyms and in the homes of my clients proved to be a laboratory for me to study the motivational level of a vast number of individuals. Sure, we hear people around us daily complaining about dealing with the same issues day in and day out and I believe that they truly want to have a different life. I would even venture to say that most people know exactly what their issues are and how to go about addressing them. I then began to ask, why not just take the big leap of faith and get on to the life they are supposed to be living? Why do they insist on living the same mundane existence year in and year out yet expect some magically different outcome to appear before their very eyes like a Chris Angel Mind- Freak episode? The more I studied people and interviewed some of the most successful people in my circumference, I learned that some people simply have a different element inside of them that separated them from their peers. At first, I had a difficult task trying explain the zeal and zest for life that the successful people had inside of them in comparison to those living the hum drum zombie lifestyle. How could these people have so much more of a natural fire blazing in their eyes than anyone else that walked into a room? Where did all the bravado, poise and boldness come from that seemed to be exuding from their pores? And then it hit me! They all knew what their KICK was in life! Some knew it at a very early age and others came upon their life's calling

14

during adulthood, but at some point, these champions all knew specifically what they were meant to do. From that point on they made a promise to themselves that they would sacrifice any and everything in their current lives to fulfill their purpose on the planet. The people that we idolize are all highly self- motivated and driven on the brink of obsession about their respective craft. The large part of the population that I have observed and had the pleasure of working with meticulously simply did not have the deep connection to their inner calling to fuel them to take the measures that would be necessary to lead them to the <u>fulfilling</u> lives that they were designed to live. This book is designed to be a guide to help you break out of your comfort zones that you've been lulled to sleep with and place you on the fast track of the fearless. Between every chapter I decided to give you a bit of bonus round by adding in some of my past writings and tips to increase your productivity and jump-start you into action. I wanted this book to be as straightforward and practical as possible. I do not want you to sit it down on a table or on the bookshelf thinking, "Man Sean really said something in that book." I want you to take massive action right away as soon as a part of a chapter speaks to you. I want you to highlight, write in the margins, take notes and make action plans as you read this work. That would be fulfilling my life's work.

Chapter 1
Finding Your One KICK!

This chapter is all about finding your focal point to invest all your time and resource into being the greatest version of yourself. The issue you will find with most "go-getters" is that our focus tends to be all over the place. We want our hands in so many things that we end up not grasping anything at all.

One of my favorite heroes in the world is the legendary Bruce Lee. Bruce Lee had the ability to captivate us with his electric martial arts movements as well as with his thought provoking quotes. One of the most memorable lines that Bruce Lee ever said was, "I fear not the man who has practiced 10,000 kicks once, but I fear the man who has practiced one kick 10,000 times. If you have ever heard of the "10,000-hour rule" by the researcher Anders Ericsson, you know that it has

been said that it takes about 10,000 hours of ultra -
focused practice to master any skill or be amongst the
top 5% of the world in said field. Bruce Lee clearly
understood the importance of mastering your craft and
having a pinpoint focus on your execution with each
and everything you do in life. To be a "Jack Of All
Trades" and "A Master Of None" has been a phrase that
has caused the downfall to so many would be greats.
What is the point in being average at best in five
different areas when you can be a stand out at one?
This comes down to having self-discipline (which we
shall cover later) and concentration on what really
means the most to you in life. You Must Discover
What Your **One KICK** Will Be In Life. By having
focus on one **KICK** I find that you can make choices
faster because right away you will know if something
falls in line with your **KICK** or if it is a total distraction

from where you are trying to go. Sometimes on the journey of life you must pass up good for great. When you have a clear-cut vision in mind of what you want to become and achieve some invitations that may sound good, but may not be in line with where you are trying to go and this will be a waste of time, money, and energy for you, which makes it totally not worth it. I would venture to say that the more success you gain over time the more shining things will pop up out of nowhere to distract you from your overarching goals. You must be like the horse on the racetrack with blinders on, only able to see straight down the track. Any slight look to your right or left can hinder you and cause you to be in last place in the race of life!

*Questions To Help You Narrow Down Your KICK *

Turn to a clean sheet of paper in your journal and write down the answer to these questions to yourself.

If money was not an issue what would you love to do daily?

- ❖ **If you suddenly had two weeks off from your current job what would you do with most that time?**
- ❖ **What type of thought energizes you upon waking?**
- ❖ **What types of positive thoughts keep you up late at night?**
- ❖ **If health were not a factor, what would you like to still be doing twenty-five years from now?**
- ❖ **What comes to you without much effort?**
- ❖ **What do other people always tell you that you are gifted at?**
- ❖ **What came to you easily as a kid?**
- ❖ **How do YOU define success?**

These are the type of questions you will need to answer within yourself to identify your one and only **KICK**. Of course, over time life will changes and people will evolve. You are not meant to be stuck in the same place you were years ago, that is a part of growth, but for the most part you want to think long and hard about your answer because this will serve as your guide for a large part of your life. All your major decisions will be based around your **KICK**. How much money you make per year, where you decide to live, who you decided to have a family with, how you spend your free time, and more importantly than all those wonderful things, your **KICK** will set the guidelines to what you absolutely will not do.

The Manifesto

About five years ago, I sat up all night reading Elliot Husle's, "Manifesto of Strength", and was totally blown away! It had me fired up and motivated. I think I must have sent that book to all the close friends in my circle at that time. I just wanted everyone to feel what I was feeling. Eventually I thought to myself, Man I need MY OWN manifesto. I decided to ask my all wise, all seeing Mentor to give me a hand with creating one. Honestly, I had never heard of the word Manifesto to this point so I clearly had no idea of how to go about creating one. I will never forget it. I went to my teacher's home as I always did and we sat on the front porch as our tradition was. We sat there and talked for about three or four hour that sunny day. We talked about what I wanted to do, my dreams, my overall aim, my past, my patterns, my behaviors, what I am most inclined to, etc. We spoke about the world, religion, politics, and various other areas of life. I was waiting for this grand large-scale manifesto? Elliot's Manifesto was about 220 pages for crying out loud. He turns to me and said, "See it...Create it...Get out of the damn way!" That was it!!!! Nothing else. What? After four hours on the porch and you got, "See it, create it, get out of the damn way?" Initially I was disappointed and in disbelief. It took a while for his real lesson to sink in. I had to soak in the power of his selective few words. I had to think back on one of my favorite African History Master Teachers Dr. Kaba, whom has appeared in the hit Documentaries Hidden Colors 1-5, Out of Darkness and Black Wall St. In one of his lectures he said that it takes a lot more intellect to be able to explain a massive thing in a few words compared to explaining something small with tons of words. He wanted me to have vision, have a goal, and have a target. He wants me to put my hands and mind to work, not just dream, but put the boots to the ground and do the grunt work of creation. Most importantly and the most difficult, get out of my own way. After the vision has been laid and the plan had been executed he wanted me to not be a roadblock to myself and let things manifest and run its course, as it should. For us Go-Getters, this will be difficult because we pride ourselves on being BEAST! We don't sit on our hands and wait for a hand out. WE MAKE IT HAPPEN. This is NOT the time for any of that. You must fall back and go into a stage of reflection and let the things that you have put out into the universe manifest back to you. When you do these three things right it seems like magic the way your goals fall into place. I have lived by this simple manifesto for all of these years and, from living by it, I have graduated college three time using this formula, married my beautiful wife and had a very beautiful wedding using this, gotten multiple jobs of different variations, given speeches that I have been paid for, competed in bodybuilding and Cross Fit competitions, and now I have writing the book you are reading all using this simple Manifesto. **Now It Is Time For You To Create Your Own Words To Live By**. Words have the power to shape the life that we live. Become the author of your life's tale and create the words that will define your mission. Dig in deep within yourself and find the magical words that speak to you the most. The phrase that sets you on fire, write it repeatedly, speak it with conviction and force, lastly, actually DO something.

The Inception Of This Book

This one story is kind of the catalyst to writing this book. I will never forget the day my wife and I went to The University of Lafayette's Library. There is no place on earth that I would rather be than at the library. figured the University's Library must surpass any public library that I have ever seen. A few of my friends that had attended this University told me that there were complete sections of just Shakespeare or other writers so in my mind they have tons of books on my favorite topic, African History! We walk into this fine establishment and it is gigantic. There were about three levels I believe. In my mind, it seems like miles of shelves filled with knowledge just calling my name. I go to the desk and ask the librarian for her African American section and I stand back and smile real bright. She goes into the computer system and click around for a bit. No answer…. Then she reached under the desk and pulls out this manual, thumbs through it, and finally points me to a direction. I get there and to my big surprise there was only a shelf and a half on my culture's history. Every book on the shelf seemed to be about slavery or the time right after it. I will never forget how upset and frustrated I felt in that moment. I felt like I could be a student at a school this big and go from my freshman year through my Doctoral degree and NOT see myself at all in these shelves in the highest light. I could not help but feel as if my small bookshelf in my "Home Of History" far surpassed this University's Library, which I'm sure they poured hundreds of thousands of dollars into. It became clear to me the only way for one to get what they really need in life is to **Do It For Yourself**. You cannot expect to get it from the school system, you cannot expect it always at a church and you cannot always look to be enlightened by certain systems that are said to be in place for your benefit. Your hunger and desire for what you yearn for has to come from within and you have to be willing to do any and everything it takes to get what you are looking for. This is how this book came about. We had a conversation about what happen to me at on UL's campus and a good buddy of mine said, "You know what, you should write a book about being as self-sufficient and self-driven." He knew of my appetite for information and the ways in which I went about feasting. I leaped at the opportunity. Let's eat up

Contributing Factors For Non-Starters

- ❖ Culture

- ❖ Social status

- ❖ Education

- ❖ Environment

- ❖ Fear

- ❖ Fear of success

(Think on ways that apply these points in life to see how they have stopped you from taking the first step).

Chapter 2

Taste Of Success

For the self-feeder the thrill of the hunt and taste of the kill (that being success) is something that consumes our thoughts day and night. It is like a person who happens to be homeless on the streets with no source of income. You feel as if you must find a way to feed yourself by ANY means. This is what your pursuit for the things you ultimately want must feel like. t does not matter what hoops you have to jump through or if the rings are on fire when you do it. **It MUST Be Done!** This is the way I have managed to reach the levels of success I have touched thus far. I had to do whatever it took to feed myself and I am speaking in terms of knowledge when I say that. I had to find ways to speak to people that you would not think to talk to. I had to find not so popular sites to buy materials from that served my purpose. I lost many hours of sleep in order to create things in the hours when I knew the world was sleep. This is the mindset and the drive of a self-feeder. Just going to your local school or organization and hope to get all of the tools you need in life to dominate is a setup for failure and disappointment in the long run.

Feed Yourself

Later on in this work I speak about the importance of investing in yourself and investing in yourself will be the main way in which you allow yourself to access the things that are you seeking for yourself. Finding the right mentors can cost at times, going to workshops and seminars in your field of study will not always be in your city and you must travel. Learning proper goal setting methods and self-assessing to put yourself back on track of your mission will all be key elements in helping you create situations where you can sustain yourself for long periods of time. Last but certainly not least you will need a healthy dose of obsession to your craft. Most times being obsessed with something is put into negative terms, but in this case you will need to have an all-time high consumption of what you are interested in because of the amount of resistance that you will face along your journey. You cannot just want to dabble with something and think that your own merit will get you to your big goals. You will have to be totally obsessed about your dreams in order to get up, brush yourself off and still think that it is the right choice to proceed further. Stay hungry my friend.

Productivity Tip
Create Your Own Rituals For Success

Most times when the word ritual is used it is taken in a very spooky way in society. By definition, a ritual is a performance of ceremonial acts prescribed by tradition or sacerdotal decree. When I say to create your own ritual for success I am telling you to study yourself and pay attention to what you did, ate, listen to, spoke to, where you performed (the environment) and most important the order in which you did it (that is the syntax) in order to replicate your success at will. Now I will be super transparent here. For some reason for the past three to four years when I go to do my school work, study, write speeches, etc. I HAVE to wear a hoodie or a long sleeve of some sort. It does not matter what time of year it is, the location, I cannot explain it, but over time it just became my thing. I kept getting A's on my papers weekly, I kept writing great speeches, so I keep doing it. If it is not broken do not fix it right? You cannot care about what others think of you and your rituals. The only thing that can be on your mind is the end result. So, tell me...What is your thing?

On the space provided below and based on what you have read so far, what are some of the things you feel are needed in order for you to achieve your personal level of success?

Chapter 3

Powering Up Your KICK
The 4 M's Of Motivation

Whether we want to admit it or not, most of us are driven by one of the 4 M's. I had never heard of the 4 M's concept before until one day I was driving for work, I overheard it on a podcast. The moment he laid out what the 4 M's entailed I instantly knew that this was a piece of groundbreaking information for me. I thought to myself how far along could I be in life had I heard of this in high school. Let us cut through the chase and let me explain to you what are the 4 M's so you can identify the one which speaks to you the most, then you can maximize it to your advantage.

The 1st M, I will speak on is Material (money, cars, homes, clothes, etc.) Because of what we are taught from childhood we think that chasing money or loving money is a bad thing. We have all heard the classic line that "Money is the root of all evil" correct? I will share with you there is nothing wrong with pursuing money if it is what makes you tick and it is what gets you out of bed at 5 A.M. ready to tackle the world! If the thought of that next car, bigger house, nice trips or paying for your children's education is the one thing that drives you like no other, use it to your advantage and set up the things in your life to revolve around money. The only advice I would offer is **IF** money is your motivation, do all you can to make IT for you and do not do anything to will hurt you or anyone else in pursuit of it. We can all think of countless celebrities and street hustlers with their cars, rims, fancy jewels and shining things. It is what drove them and made taking chances worth it for them right or wrong.

The next M is speak on will be Mating (aka the pursuit of the opposite sex). Now this M may seem like it is flat out geared toward the fellas, but times have changed so much these days the ladies want the same things as well so it applies to both genders. The person driven by the opposite sex wants nothing more than to have groups of suitors hanging off of them every second they can. This very thought drives them to practice harder and dedicate themselves to their craft with no restrictions whatsoever. These types of people pride themselves on their sexual conquest. We can easily close our eyes and picture the athletes and entertainers with countless fans at their beck and call day in and day out. Unfortunately, we also know how many of these great figures let their M get them into tons of trouble in their personal and business lives. You must be careful once again when you burn out your desires within using your M to achieve your dreams do not let your desires burn YOU.

The third M is for Mastery! I feel that this is my most favorite and personal M to be honest with you. The people that are driven by Mastery pride themselves on being the very best at their respect craft. The Mastery driven person may be big on status. They want to be the doctor, the lawyer, the mathematician, and the scientist. I'll go specific with people such as Kobe Bryant, Michael Jordan, Floyd Mayweather, Oprah Winfrey, Steve Job. These people had large sums of money flow into their hands, but the material was a byproduct of their drive for the Mastery of their particular craft. One of my main warnings to the Mastery driven person would be to **NOT** lose your love ones in the course of your pursuit of your craft as it can become very easy to get lost in your training, your study, your research etc. Remember it is very lonely at the top if you do not take your love ones along with you for the journey. As with all things in life, balance is key.

The last of the 4 M's is Momentum. This type of person almost goes totally against my Finding Your KICK chapter, but having their hands in as many things as possible drives them. I think this type of person may be driven by STARTING things and never finishing them. They want to bounce around from one thing to the next. Once again I am not here to judge and there are millions of roads to success. If you are driven in this form or fashion, by all maximize it! If the thought of starting that next business, changing a major in school, totally taking up a new craft sends electricity through your body, DO IT!

Now that we have a better understanding of what each of the 4 M's are, I want you to once again honestly ask you what is it that fires you up? I find the answer to this question very empowering so much so that once you know, operate from a much more power place. Keep in mind there is no right or wrong answer and yes, some people can have different levels and combinations of the 4 M's.

Questions of Interest

❖ **What is your sole motivation?**

❖ **Explain why?**

❖ **At what point in life did you realize this?**

❖ **Can you name points in your life where this was evident to you?**

You Cannot Be Extraordinary Being Ordinary

When you really want success, your definition of "normal" totally changes.

Your lunch breaks are no longer a time to sit back with a meal and talk the talk with coworkers and friends. You do not get full nights of sleep. You make the assertive effort to squeeze the most out of each and every hour of the day because you know that time is more precious than money to a self-feeder. You can always make money back, but time, time you can never recapture. TV...If you are a self-feeder you might as well just pawn it. No time to sit and watch brainless shows that will most likely add no value to your life or get you closer to your goal. For advanced self-feeders in my power circle, to sit and watch an entire movie or TV show is like going to an exotic island. You cannot be as successful as you want to be watching all of the TV shows, games, every club night or attend every birthday party. In essence there has to be sacrifice involved. Stick to your goals and give yourself something real to celebrate. Most people that party all of the time do not have anything tangible or have merit to party about whatsoever.

Chapter 4

Stubborn Goals / Flexible Methods

When I was a child I am sure that any family member and former teacher will tell you that I was a pretty bull headed and stubborn child. I was never disrespectful or an outright bad boy by any means, but when I was set on something and I wanted it to be a certain way good luck in getting me to change my mind to see it your way. Of course, as a kid you are supposed to do exactly what the grown-ups say, not challenge it- and if you do you will find yourself in a lot of trouble. Thankfully I never got into major trouble growing up at home, school or with the law, but I am sure I gave some of the adults in my life high blood pressure to say the least. I find that as an adult, this same bull-headedness has turned into one of my greatest superpowers in my repertoire. I just flat out will not quit on the things that I pursue until I see them to completion. One valuable lesson that I have learned along the way with wisdom is that your end result may not come in the exact form in which you envisioned it in your goal setting process, but it will come! **You** must be aware when it comes. You have to grow to be a result driven person. Remember do not get so hung up on the "how". (How this gone happen? How that gone happen, etc.)

Once you have clearly identified your one KICK in life and have done your work, goal-setting and action planning (a major part in seeing your vision through) will be grit work. A lot of times some of your greatest oppositions against what you are trying to do will come in the form of family and friends who, for the most part mean well for you. They think they are doing you a favor by shielding you from possible heartache, lost funds, lost time, etc. Sad to say that a lot of these people are trying to set limitations on you based on what they either could not do themselves or based on their personal fears they are projected onto you. This is a moment where your stubbornness and self-confidence with the belief in what you are doing will come in handy. It will be very hard for most to dig in deep to go against the wishes of your love ones to make **YOUR** dream come true. However, It is **YOUR** responsibility to make **YOUR** dreams manifest, but only **YOU** and can see **YOUR** dream the way that you do. YOU must have total belief in **YOURSELF** and **YOUR** abilities. **YOU** must almost air on the side of cockiness at times for your own sake. **YOU** will need to feed the belief in **YOURSELF** until the world has no choice but to believe in you. Also, we must factor in that from the moment you conceive an idea in your mind to its completion you will have challenges. There is no telling what challenge you may face along the way and I will speak on overcoming obstacles later in this book, but my point to you at this moment is you will need perseverance like you have never seen before to take those kinds of punches square on the chin and say yes, it is still worth it press on. People will point the finger at you and give you the "I told you so speech" as a result; you must have thick skin and not miss the message they are trying to tell you. Do not waste your precious time and resource feeding into someone else's negativity, but be flexible enough to adjust your methods accordingly. You must cultivate a mindset that serves YOUR purpose at all times. Now I must warn you that most of the most successful people in their respectful craft are often times called cocky, jerk, arrogant and the list goes on, but to me it is a sign that they have fully mastered this principle already and they will not let outside comments distract them from their dreams. I would rather be a successful jerk than a nice bum any day, believe that!

"Man is what he BELIEVES " -Anton Chekhov

Questions of Interest

❖   Was there a point in your life where you wish that you could've been a bit more stubborn?

❖   How have you historically responded to resistance in your life?

❖   Do you find yourself occupied trying to please others are remain in their favor, if so why?

Remember, these questions and notes are the real gems of this book. The more honest you can be with yourself the better.

Productivity Tip
The Relaxation Warrior

One of the things about being a warrior is that most of us make the mistake of priding ourselves on the amount of work we can do without rest. We love to speak about how we do not sleep and how hard we press on the weekends while the competition has their feet up. That is all fine and dandy, but we must remember to keep all things in balance. Your nervous system can only take so much and I know most of us are overdosing on caffeine of some sort do not lie) that taxes our nerves and never give us a chance to rest and recover as the body was designed to do. The same way we are hard set on our work and goals we must be hard set on times of relaxation and rest. One day a week I would suggest taking a break from social media. You may not realize it, but every time you are tuned into social media it is taxing your nerves on a small level. Especially with all of the things that can potentially become stressful or an excitement trigger. Unless your job demands it, I would also suggest taking a few days away from your email or just checking it once per day instead of 30 times a day. Schedule a few days away from the stressors of your home environment and if you can afford it, eliminate stressful people out of your life. Whether it is family members or friends, it does not mean not communicating with these people any more, it simply means not giving them your energy. Take a small break for a couple of hours and be as non-productive as possible on purpose. If you listen to audiobooks and or podcasts as much as I do, you may also take a few days just listening to some music or not listening to anything. I know these days it can be hard to find *music that you want to hear, but it is vital for your recovery process. I also know that most of us in this demographic probably barely and rarely ever go out and that is by design. It could do you some good to get dressed and step out a weekend per month maybe. Put down your swords. Take off your bulky shields. Enjoy the people around that you bang so hard for in the first place physically and psychologically. Next week go back to war a better warrior fighting for Love!*

Chapter 5

Find Yourself A Mentor (The Master)

I know without a doubt one of the key factors in the success that I have had so far in my life training wise, relationship, fatherhood, business, academic, and mentoring wise are all due to my ability to humble myself and actively seek out advice from those that I know are skillful in that particular walk of life. Without proper guidance, I do not know where I would be in life right now and I would have spent years bumping my head against unnecessary walls just to make small measures of progress. The day my mentor stepped into my life and started to pour into me for hours on end weekly my life started to change almost overnight it seem. It is not easy to find a mentor in this busy and hectic world that we live in. It is well worth your trouble to speed up your progress to get to the next level of living when you find your mentor.

Some people feel as if they are "know it all's." You know the type. They figure there is nothing under the sun that they cannot figure out on their own. They figure they have had some levels of success in another part of life so they arrogantly and wrongly assume they will automatically find success in the next endeavor they decide to take on. I cannot explain to you how detrimental that form of thinking can be. Once you have identified your one **KICK** in life, you have created your goal / action list, the very next thing I advise you to do is find yourself a person in that field that is already performing at a high level to guide you. You want to find a mentor that can tell you all about the many pitfalls they had to go through so you eliminate the simple mishaps in the beginning of your journey. You want to hear all of the things they wish they could do if they had the chance to do it again. More importantly, you want the "cheat codes"! That is right. Life is about working smarter and not harder than the next man. You want all the "hacks" possible to help you spring pass your peers on the road to victory lane. Make sure that you find a mentor who is brutally honest with you and gives you constructive criticism, but they are also mindful about how they handle and treat you. Find a guide that will be there in your times of darkness because the dark days will come, you WILL question yourself and you will feel as if no one else around understands your battles. Your mentor will be that guiding light and the push in the back that you need to get you out of the mud and back on solid land. In order to find the ultimate gold you must find someone who pushes you beyond your limitations. You need someone who will hold you to a higher standard and demand more from you than you will demand from yourself.

You may think to yourself, "Well Sean how does one go about finding a mentor?" I would say if you are a current student, seek counsel in a teacher or other parts of the staff that you admire and respect enough to share your dream with. You can even find a mentor in a coach if you play sports to help you on and off the field of play. If you are out of school, I would say look at some of the community leaders in your area or maybe the local church you attend. If none of these methods work for you, take advantage of the information highway that we are a part of these days called the Internet. You can easily look up people you admire online and even find the means to contact them via social media or their direct email address if provided. I can say from my experiences some people are easier to speak to than you think and my experience has also taught me that people in the know most times love to share their knowledge. They love to pour into people who are eager to learn! I will also share with you the fact your mentor does not have to speak to you at all for you to learn from them. You can learn a ton from watching YouTube clips of all the greats; you can find old books and letters that have been written many years ago. Even if the person has passed, their message is still here to be a guide for the generations to come learn their lessons and act on their wisdom they left with us. It only serves them right if we execute on it.

Things To Keep In Mind As A Mentee

Once you have secured a mentor to guide you on your path, there are a few things you want to keep in mind to ensure you get the most out of your experience, as this is a two-way street. My first suggestion would be to bring something to the table because everything in the universe is about you get out of a situation what you put into it. Find a way in which your mentor feels as if you are adding value to their lives as well. This cannot be a one-sided affair. The expression says that steel sharpens steel so you must provide some form of benefit to your teacher. When you are around your mentor ask as many questions as possible and make sure they are in a non-aggravating manner. You want to let your teacher know you are the willing student and you are there to soak up every drop of what they have to offer. At the same time, you don't want to come off as a nuisance as this could drive them away. Next, if your mentor gives you things to do or something to go and research make sure you use instant application and report back to them what it is that you experience from their information. This will let them know you are serious and not just there to waste their time and energy. The more you prove you will actually use their information, the more they will want to pour into you. Keep in mind; your mentor is only acting as a guide for you. He is not supposed to DO anything for you what so ever and there will be no magic out of the sky moment just because you found yourself a very high level person to align yourself with. It will still take tons of flat out effort on your part to make all the advice that he is giving to you manifest in your reality. You can get all of the advice on the planet from all of the best teachers, but until you actually apply their principles it is all for naught. My next piece of advice would be to use simple science in your favor. We all have mirror neurons, which allow us to learn things by just simply being in the presence of it, like a baby copying your facial expression though they don't know what they mean. Spend as much time in person with your teacher as possible. Try to take in every single small detail about your teacher and their life, study how they are with different types of people, learn how they are with their personal life, learn how they operate and move. This person is supposed to be like you looking at yourself in the future. Pick up all that you can and use what you can now to accelerate your process. My last piece of advice would be to always give props and thanks to your teacher by showing appreciation and honoring them for doing such a life service for which you could never pay back. This is the way to grow a healthy mentor to mentee relationship in which both of you grow and develop for years to come.

"The Student repays the master poorly if he only remains a student. "

Points to consider

❖   How much do you think you could improve your life with the help of a mentor?

❖   Gather a list of 5 people that you may feel are out of your reach, find a way to contact them. Be creative by using email, social media or Google to gather their contact information etc.

❖   Who are some leaders from the past that may not be here anymore that you can research their work?

Eye Of The Tiger

When you are trying to achieve your goals, this eye of the tiger is what you need. It is hard to capture in words, I do not know what to call it and from the looks of things, some have it while others do not. I known it can be honed and learned like any other skill. It is the raw ability to separate yourself from your conscious mind, and it is the ability to push yourself even when you absolutely do not want to. No matter how early you have to get up or no matter your lack of sleep. Dig down deeper into this thing and pull from its...source. You are on empty. Your mind cannot help you and you cannot count on your emotional state to pull you through at this point, you must trust yourself and have discipline enough to KNOW that your success is on the other side of your fear. That Eye of the Tiger man.

"Everybody wants to be a beast until it's time to do what beast do!" -Eric Thomas, The Motivator

Chapter 6

Always Invest In Self

The perfect follow up to finding your mentor is applying the concept of investing in yourself. Yes, there are tons of people out there with loads of information just waiting to pour into a willing student. For you though, you must to be willing to pay the price for the years they have invested in what they do. If a guy has gone to school for years and spent thousands of dollars, he is in his right to want to demand five thousand or more for his services, do you agree? I make this example to speak about the importance of being willing to invest in yourself in order to be the most efficient individual. On the path of doing things for yourself you should not expect a bunch of handout to drop into your lap out of the sky. Some of the most valuable nuggets that you will need in your arsenal will not be in plain sight either. You will have to pay the price for them. It is a universal law in fact; you will get back exactly what you put out into the universe. Nothing more. Nothing less.

Why You Should Invest In Yourself

As if you need a reason to invest in yourself, the best answer would be that YOU matter! The first Law Of Nature is Self Preservation, which means, Do For Self. You have to take care of yourself before you can take care of your spouse, your children or any person in the community. Until you are in a good place you are of no service to anyone else. It may seem selfish on the surface level and maybe this is the reason why you have not invested in yourself in the past, but understand by being slightly selfish for the moment you can improve the lives of the people around you for a lifetime. Hear me out, as a person who is trying to be the greatest form of himself, one of the main things you must keep in mind is that you will have to go out and hunt down most of the things you need and want. Nobody else is responsible to make it happen for you.

Second of all, nobody else outside of you will care about any of your goals the way you do; not your spouse, your kids, or your parents. They all love you, but if you get a Ph.D. or not it will not matter to them in the grand scheme of things as It is all on YOU to make it a reality.

How To Invest In Yourself

Of course you have endless ways in which you choose to invest in yourself. One of the best methods that I have heard was to invest 3% of your income for the year into self-help books, workshops, boot camps, seminars, coaching etc. So if you make $30,000 a year, you would invest $300 in that year towards improving yourself. Now the payoff from that will be three to five times greater than the investment. From that point the following year, you can do the same thing again or as you earn more money from your previous improvements, you can increase your percentage to reflect the increase in income, as this will increase the amount of improvement you see in your life and your bottom line. The method you chose does not really matter. The main thing is that you get started working on yourself and being more proactive about your success. You can start going to a few sites where you find free PDF books or free online classes to get your feet wet. You can go on Amazon or Kindle and find a wealth of books or products that cost under $3.00. You can go into your smart phone and get a Podcast App and get thousands of hours of information for free as well. The main thing is that once your ball is rolling you continue to feed into it and the leaps and bounds that you will experience will surpass any words that I could fit into this book.

<u>RE</u>-Invest In Yourself

Ok, so you have learned all about investing in
yourself and you have made some progress. Chapter
over right...WRONG! This is not a one-time buy in.
After you have invested in yourself and made some
pay off the best thing to do next is to repeat the process
immediately, investing more into you! That is right
investing more! The more you put into yourself, the
higher you percentage payout will be. My suggestion
would be when you start to plan your year in January,
add into your calendar some dates to attend seminars in
your field. Look up online webinars you can take part
in once a quarter. Possibly find some lower level
classes in your city or nearby you can attend to
increase your skillset in a certain area. Yearly as your
income increases, you should increase your percentage
investment into yourself.

Points of Interest

❖ How can you begin investing in yourself at this moment?

❖ How much are you willing to invest into your development and growth?

❖ How far are you willing to travel to learn something?

❖ What are you willing to give up to achieve your dreams?

❖ How much are you willing to pay for coaching?

❖ How many weekends are you willing to sacrifice in order to develop yourself?

Productivity Tip
Take Massive Action

One of the most important lessons I have learned from the Strength Coach Zach Evn-sh is the principle of taking Massive Action in life at whatever it is you want to do. You cannot tip toe your way to success, you cannot dabble and stumble upon victory, You have to be a taker, You must demand it and be bold enough to take all comers as it will not come in a pretty little package nor will it be a walk in the park. It will not just fall into your lap by osmosis, you will want to quit at times, and you will doubt yourself. No one around you will care about your dream as much as YOU DO, and they should not because after all, this is YOUR goal, not anyone else's. That thought is scary to some people and keeps them paralyzed in their tracks.

Somehow I find it empowering that you get to write your own story as well as create your own destiny.

So many times, year after year we see so many people make all of these New Year Resolutions and plans with no intention to make one step into making their dream manifest in reality. FORGET THAT! This is why I do not believe in making New Year Resolutions. What can you do about your dream right now, today? What phone calls can you make? Is there someone or a business you can email right now as we speak? Want to change your eating? Do it in the very next meal. Want to run a 5-K? Try to at least walk somewhere short right now and get your feet on the road. The most important thing is starting the process of putting your mind and body in motion because this will give you the extra energy you need to tackle your goal. Once you have started you will be amazed with the generated momentum, which will assist you in increasing the likelihood of your overall success. Make your next move, your best move.

Chapter 7
Reverse Engineering Your Goals

One of the biggest things I have ever experienced in life was competing in the 2013 Mr. Louisiana Bodybuilding Show. This was hands down one of the most physically challenging goals I have ever tackled in my life and it took every single ounce of heart, willpower, character, and grit to make it all become reality. The one element that it took was my nutrition coach's ability to know where he wanted me to be in July and understand how to scientifically break that down into micro chunks to tell me exactly what to eat week-by-week starting in DECEMBER! No easy task right, but with his "know how" and my ability to remain coachable and stick to his plan, I got on stage that night 35lbs. (lighter) than when I started in

December. My waist was back to my Jr. High days, and my body fat was under 9%! I came in 3rd place in my weight class. That journey was one that my family and myself will never forget for all times as I learned a valuable lesson within that process which goes beyond how much fat is in a slice of toast at the waffle house. This how to Reverse Engineer your goals in order to know exactly what you need to do from day to day, week to week and so on until you have made your fantasy manifest in this reality. Let us it break it down.

Going Into The Future

Within the very first step of Reverse Engineering your goals you see the importance of establishing what your KICK will be. What IS YOUR GOAL? What are you trying to do here? The 1st thing that we want to do in this process is sit where we are now with what we have and go into the future in our mind. We want to dream big. Imagine that money is not an issue and you have access to any resource that you want. This type of thinking is needed to help clearly define what you want and how your needs will get met. The answer to this question will serve as a lighthouse guiding you on your path to greatness. I will make up a goal just for example purposes.

One Bite At A Time

Let us say that I want to successfully graduate with my Master's degree in less than two years. I would write it out on the top of my paper. The next step would be to speak to my school advisor and find out how many classes or credits I will need to complete this degree (Let us say 12-15 classes for the sake of the example.) I need to ask, "Do I have to take breaks between classes or can I take my classes in a back to back fashion which helps me cut my overall time down? How many weeks are the classes (Let us say it's 6 week courses.) I need to make sure that the classes I enroll in are on par with my major and not just filler classes. After I get the feedback on the variables, I can now take out a planner and chart my course from the first day of class all the way to graduation day to see exactly how long that will take."

Now I know month to month exactly what class I will have at that time and I will know how to plan my personal and social life AROUND this for the next two years to come.

You see how having your goal firmly in your mind protects you from the things you should NOT be doing because it go against the vision? "Do not let the distractions distract you!" Back to the example, "I know exactly when my finals weeks are. I can even make out a plan week by week of what I need to get done in what order to make sure that I successfully pass all of my courses because having to repeat a failed class goes against the two -year goal." As you can see from the example above, I just charted out a person's course from day one, calling a school advisor, to the person graduating and crossing the stage, and finally releasing balloons with their loved ones! This process can be done with any goal you can think of. Keep the end in mind and mentally work backward to the present and you will know exactly what you should and should NOT be doing in your day to day life.

Points of Interest

❖ The extra credit work is straightforward in this chapter. I provided a detailed example of how I would go about Reverse Engineering my goals in the previous section. Now pick a goal, put your pen to paper, look into your future and work your way back!

❖ You want to write in as many vivid details as possible. Use all of your senses, as you want to be able to hear it, feel it, smell it, and taste your goal.

Chapter 8
The Ability To Self-Assess

One of the major downfalls to being successful is the lack of the ability to self-assess. So many times, we find certain levels of victory in one area of our lives and get too excited about the fact that we think we can tackle any challenge that may come our way with the same methods as this is one of the most important aspects to realize. Every situation will not require the same methods to achieve success. You must keep an extremely critical eye on yourself at all times and you must cultivate the ability to hold a mirror to yourself and be honest about the reflection you see. Not only what you see, but also the direction in which you see yourself going. My most recent example of having to self-assess came during my last statistics class I had to take for my Master's Degree. In 95% of my college classes I just blew them away without much effort. I was known for making A's and B's in my sleep. All of the popping bottles and celebrating stopped the moment I saw my transcript, I then realized my next course would be a six weeks course on the use of statistics in Behavioral Sciences. My heart dropped instantly. I was known for being pretty good with my words, not to mention I can write a paper in APA format without much effort at this point in my college career, but what it came down to was that Mathematics was my Kryptonite. I knew how to read class material ahead of time, how to take proper notes, how to study exactly what the assignment called for, but I did not do as well in Mathematics. For the first time in my life I could not out muscle this issue, I could not will myself through it and I could not-manipulate one variable in my favor. After the first two weeks of receiving failing grades, I had to admit to myself the ugly truth. At this rate, I was on a fast track to failing this class, which was a required class to graduate. I would have to pay the total sum of $1,200 back for the class, which was unacceptable. I had to humble myself, make as many phones as I could to all my college grad friends to see if anyone could help me with this Statistics class. After what seemed like days of phone calls and texts I was blessed to hunt down a childhood friend who happens to be a genius. Over the remaining four weeks of class I had to drive an hour to his home, meet for three to four hours at a time to get my assignments done. I passed the course with a D, but I indeed passed. At that time I only had three remaining classes to pass in order to cross the graduation stage with a Master's in Psychology. Had I remained hard headed and thought to myself, "Hey you make A's weekly in any other class" I would have surely failed the class and would have been further away from achieving my academic goal.

"Your success has defeated you"

-Bane (Villain in Batman Dark Knight)

Mirror, Mirror On The Wall

The most important thing needed in order to "self-assess" is the ability to look at the truth about what you are doing and how well you are really doing it. Do not attempt to pretty it up, do not add sprinkles and do not try to search for the silver lining. Simply ask yourself, "Is what you have been doing effective and is it producing the fruit that you are seeking?" If not, it is really time to recalibrate and adjust your game plan. Often times when we have been successful, we are used to the pats on the back and the at-a-boys and we start to believe all of the hype that surrounds us. Our friends and family mean well and they love us, but at a certain point we have to really ask ourselves, "Is this current thing that I am doing really for me, or am I over rating my abilities?" It takes a very strong and brave person to be honest enough to look directly into the mirror, examine what they see and accept exactly who and what they see.

Back To Your Drawing Board

If you have actually followed along, have been making notes, answering the question asked of you, it is imperative that you see the importance of this particular section. If you have identified your "KICK" in life, reverse engineered your goals, found a mentor to guide and HELP YOU direct your life, you now have the opportunity to go back to the drawing board to compare where you are now versus what your initial goals were. This is like taking a trip with a GPS System, visually seeing yourself navigate the desired course. In the event you deviate from your path, reroute yourself back to the drawing board to make adjustments accordingly.

Is this new venture in line with your natural gifts, talents and skillsets? Once again be honest, was this even your idea? I know at times when you have some level of success, people appear from all directions with things THEY think would be great for you. Once again, they probably mean well, but this is not for you and you must turn away as soon as possible. Have you consulted your mentor or your support team about this? Hopefully they are strong enough as well as love you enough to be honest with you to get you back on the original path.

Make The Adjustments

After you have looked at yourself in the mirror and have gone to the drawing board, what is next and maybe the only thing left to do is take massive action to see yourself achieve small levels of success which allows you to build your confidence in order to continue achieving success. We all look for the major accomplishments not realizing that by focusing on what we think are small victories is the key to great levels of success. Now let me say this, MAYBE you are on the right path, MAYBE you need a change in perspective and MAYBE you need to push harder, but you DEFINITELY need a coach/mentor/advisor to assist in getting you through the upcoming challenges. The next move should be executing whatever it is that you have identified as holding you back. There is no other option; this is not about whining, complaining or being EMOTIONAL about it. It is ok to not do so well at something, but once you have examined it, either you take the proper action to improve in this department or move on for good.

"Know when to hold'em, know when to fold'em"

-Kenny Rogers

Points of Interest

❖   To this point in your life's journey what are some of the adjustments that   you can make right away?

❖   When you look at your work performance, relationships, social life, family, school, etc in what ways can you admit that you have not been giving 100%?

❖   In what ways have you lied to yourself about your life's reflection in the mirror and more importantly why did you feel the need to lie? You have to face the music.

Chapter 9
Show Discipline

When you have mastered the ability to self-assess, and as you have committed to your chosen KICK, the next most important quality to possess is **Discipline.** Earlier in this work I mentioned my experience as a bodybuilder and that I also competed in the Cross Fit Open. In both of these physical endeavors, I had to exhibit the greatest levels of Discipline that I have ever summoned within myself. Discipline is the ultimate test between YOU and YOU! It is easy at times to deny other people from certain things they may want from you, but it is extremely difficult to deny yourself things within your own power. When you take on these types of extreme physical challenges, you MUST go out and find yourself a coach to guide you along. Their job is to use their knowledge in the particular field of study they are in and help you to build a plan of action. Once you all build and agree on that plan, the journey is totally up to YOU to walk the path YOURSELF.

When I chose to compete in both sports, my coach did not live around me nor was there anyone there to make sure I did my cardio at certain times of night, counting my calories for me, and surely no one to lift all those weights all of those hundreds of hours that I spent punishing my body. The only way I could get those challenges done was through my level of Self-Discipline. There is one thing about the sport of bodybuilding unlike any other sport is that you are not clashing against other men physically like in football or basketball. This sport is all about the person that stuck to their diets the best, the longest, the most planned out, who did their cardio and did not cut corners. Who really did all of the extra hours of posing in their free time? When you are on stage with nothing else but trunks on in front of hundreds of strangers, literally being judged which is most people's worst fear, you surely appreciate how disciplined you have been over months of training or you feel the sick pain of regret in your gut from knowing that you cut corners and did not give 100% effort to your dreams. In this sport, "To the disciplined go the spoils!"

Embrace Sacrifice

One of the main tips that I would give to any person asking how to be more disciplined in their lives would be to "Embrace The Sacrifice." Discipline, in a lot of ways requires a person to deny themselves of things they hold near and dear to their hearts. Food, soda, smoking, sex, drinking, video games, sports programming, sleep, you name it. The name of this game is to refrain! It will not be easy and it will not be pretty, but once you DECIDE and COMMIT to a certain path, you should acknowledge that you would not be able to do what you have been doing to obtain the things you ultimately want. You must embrace the things you are giving up as simply being part of the process. For some of the things you are giving up, "depending on the type of goal you have set ", will only be temporary. Example being four years for a degree is temporary. Maybe you train and diet for-six months to a year to change your body equals temporary. Perhaps you must become more strict spending wise allowing time to build your credit for a car or a home, whatever it is will not last forever if you wish to partake in these activities once you have accomplished your goal. This is another way to manipulate your mind into doing what needs to be done in the moment by giving yourself a timeline on your discipline. I hear that in fasting for spiritual growth, a person is supposed to pray and thank the Most High or their god when those hunger pains hit them to keep it on the front of their conscious why they are fasting. I would advise to employ this same tactic in other areas in your life. While you are getting the urge to repeat some past activity detrimental to your goals, think to yourself why you are in this place you find are in now, what is the reward at the end of the journey?

Submerge Yourself In Your Craft

One of the main suggestions I can make to anyone when it comes to increasing their discipline toward their goal would be to submerge themselves into what they are pursuing. When I was preparing for my bodybuilding competition, I covered every inch of my room with pictures of bodybuilders from magazines, posters, and sticky notes with motivational quotes. I had my trunks for show night six months in advance thanks to my wife. There was not one inch in the room where my eyes fell and did not land on something motivational to me for the next meal or the next workout. Of course my personal story may be extreme to some, but you cannot visit your goal a couple of times a week and expect greatness. You must have things around you at every turn that forces you to connect to your purpose until you see the mission is complete. I did this same method in high school, as a basketball player where my room became a shrine to the basketball gods was hoop worship for me. I guess you can say that Visualization has always been a big thing for me before I was aware of the science or the power behind its use. Once in a speech I gave to troubled youth, I asked them one by one what did they want to be in life as they gave me their long range of answers. Next, I asked them if I were to have a hidden camera following them for the previous week, how many hours per week would I see them actually engaging in what they said they wanted to be? Not one hand went up and at that point in the presentation, my point was clear. You cannot say out of your mouth you want to be an artist, yet you never ever draw or paint anything. You have no work to produce, nor do you own any art utensils. I believe you and it ONLY sounds good to you! Ask yourself if there were a camera following you all last week what would we see?

Make It A Lifestyle

My next suggestion is to make your goal a lifestyle so that the Discipline you need to exhibit is second nature and not something that you have to spend so much energy to force yourself to do. Many of your goals will be fairly small time wise, you will only need to show discipline for a few months to a year at most. Other goals you want to achieve may take a lifetime to manifest as this requires you to change your into a brand new being. This will demand you reinvent the way you do things for the rest of your life. In order to be the supreme version of yourself will require every single detail of your life is done with a purpose that is well thought out. You may need to drastically change the time you are accustomed to going to bed at night or you may need to wake up hours earlier to get ahead of the curve. You may also need to permanently let go of some of your meals, or introduce new foods into your diet you may have vowed to never eat in the past. You must be willing to adjust any and everything in your current life in order to get what YOU said you wanted with no questions asked. This is the "Sweet Spot" in the Discipline arena. When you get to the point where going to the gym is happening as unconsciously as you brush your teeth, THEN you have done something. At the time when I was at my physical best, I almost hated to get the compliment that I was a very disciplined person because of time I stayed in the gym, why you may ask, I LOVED every moment of it. At this point it was smooth, easy, and my ideal place to be. Discipline for me at this time was paying my bills on time or turning in college assignments. Being in the gym was a given to me as I felt I did not deserve a pat on the back for something I could do in my sleep. I realize in hindsight I was mistaken as I missed a key element in the middle of the hustle and bustle of life. I had successfully cultivated a way to make fitness not just a pastime for me, but also a full lifestyle. When you reach a point in your life where you can make your Discipline a lifestyle, there are automatic built in boundaries. When you have a lifestyle, there are obvious things that you will and will not take part in because of the commitment to your new choices will make being Disciplined easier for you-versus a person that is casually pursuing something. Keep in mind, we are creators and we can make our lives into whatever it is we want them to be TODAY! Make a choice and commit.

*** Questions To Consider***

❖ What are some things in your life you know are holding you back from being the greatest version of yourself?

❖ How long can you go without the things you listed in the previous Question 1?

❖ What kind of plan can you create in order to help you start to wean off some of your vices that are holding you back?

❖ Names some areas in your life where a lack of discipline has hurt you?

❖ Name some things in your life that would likely increase if you had more discipline? Think about your health, relationships, occupation, and lifestyle.

"You do not decide your future, you decide your habits and your habits decide your future."

What Is The Point Of Being Normal?

Consider this, every Sunday millions of "normal" people (fans) spend their hard-earned money to pack themselves into expensive stadiums in order to watch a few "abnormal" people (the football players) play the American game of Football. Now mind you all of the abnormal people get the big money contracts, the Nike shoe deals, the Gatorade commercials and all of the spoils of being a high- profile person. So, tell me once again why do you want to fit in so bad? What is the real benefit from being normal? Now, do not miss the lesson in this passage. I am not telling you to go out and try to be an NFL player. What I AM telling you is, you may want to consider the time, practice and discipline these high- level performers put into their craft. Think of the things most of these people give up for most of their lives in order to live like kings now.

Think of the premium these guys place on excellence in everything they do in order to stand out amongst their peer base. Take on these same types of attributes to your daily life; make the proper adjustments to discipline yourself from certain pleasures for the overall goal. Make it a point to be the absolute best on your job and in other parts of your life, before you know it you will enjoy the spoils of being a champion on your own scale.

Chapter 10
Still Kicking!!!
Overcoming Obstacles

We have always heard everything happens in life in its ordained time. Of course, you would not know this by the time you see this complete work in its finished format, but I wrote this book chapter by chapter out of standard order on purpose. My point in this chapter is there could be no better time to write about overcoming obstacles than right now with the type of catastrophe that has taken place in my family in this present moment. There is no need for the details of the recent events in this work, but there is no greater setback than loss of life in any person's life. Nothing can derail you from your plans, goals and dreams like suddenly losing a loved one and the emotional, psychological trauma that will follow said event. All in all, when the dust settles you find out very quickly that life must go on for the living. The people at your job will understand, but at some point, they will expect you to come back and get on the clock. Your bills will not stop because you are at your lowest point, your friends and other members of your family will be on the next thing after they finish patting your back and telling you how much " it is going to be alright." With that being said, we must find a way to pull ourselves out of the dark cloak of despair and get back on the path to glory in our own unique ways.

Life Challenges

On your road to finding your KICK, slaying your goals like dragons, there WILL BE challenges in every direction you turn. Over the course of penning this book I have had to write in some of the weirdest environments in order to get this done. I have been in the back of restaurants, on the side of truck stops, in between sessions with clients, writing at odd times of night, writing when I should be doing my Master's degree work, when I should be doing my documentation for my job, while missing things that most people take pleasure in. It takes a real "by any means" mindset to get what you want. You must be a taker and you have to pick spots in life to be selfish by putting all others on the side for a short period of time in order to get your task done. Believe me, your goals matter to YOU more than anyone else on the planet.

Do not expect people to understand your time; do not wait for people or life to make a perfect window of time for you to quietly do your craft. This dreamland does not exist; you must carve it out for yourself, as this is a major key in maintaining your KICK in life. We do not wait until something is given to us, we take it, aggressively!

Two Choices

In life there will be challenges and roadblocks; the most important thing to keep in mind is that you have Two Choices after a challenge shows up in your life. You can stay down in the dumps about whatever your roadblock maybe and fold, or you can put your eyes back on what is important to you and slowly introduce yourself back to your craft. We have seen it time again, the people raised in some of the most poverty stricken circumstances somehow rise above their peers who are in the same circumstances. They are the outliers compared to the rest of their environment as you may wonder to yourself how in the world did they become larger than life out of a situation that was so small. The answer is clearly in the choices they made for themselves coupled with the life they wanted to live. This same mindset can be seen in the people that overcome hard times in life due to their refusal to lie down no matter the circumstance. It does not matter how many things are stacked against them, great players feel like if there is still any time left on the clock, they can get the ball and WIN the game - the game of life that is. When you find yourself down in life you must tap back into why you chose this particular KICK for yourself. You have to reconnect to your motivations and drives while you feel as if all is lost and nothing is going your way. You must remember to take the road back one step at a time not expecting to operate at 100% after times of trauma. The more you can move towards a progressive direction, the faster you can get back to your higher self. Maybe you start off getting back to the environment where you use to go for creativity sitting there not forcing yourself to produce anything, just getting back to your basics. Moreover, the progression is simply putting on an outfit that makes you feel confident on the inside and taking a small walk. What is important is, it does not matter how small of a start you make, and the point is that you start again. I cannot promise you that it will be perfect or that your life will be back to the same level, but you must press forward and you cannot allow yourself to get stuck in the quicksand of depression knowing you can take back control over your life.

Your Goals Are A Matter Of Life Or Death

The main way to persevere through hard times is to look at achieving your goal as if it is a matter of life and death. You have to have the aggressive mentality as if your next meal depended on you completing the next step in your daily activities. While writing this book, there was not an actual deadline, no company calling me weekly to make sure I was still writing, nor did I have a major PR team pushing me along the way. When I started this mission I told myself that I would imagine a major publishing company wanting to do a book deal with me in a certain amount of months. I forced a hard deadline on myself that I actually made the time restriction almost impossible to meet making it harder for me to procrastinate. I cannot begin to tell you how many things came up over the course of writing this work, but the main thing that got me through is that I kept my focus on writing in spots as if I had no other choice in the world. Even the days I did not want to write or felt I wanted to slack off and kick back with a novel to read (which is my favorite past time) I forced myself to at least plan out the next chapter I would write in the next session. You have to kick it in overdrive or die trying as losing is not an option for the self-motivated. Every person you love and hold dear is counting on you to live up to your full potential because the next meal is on you! You can fall back and starve or have the spoils of a king based on the actions you take right now.

*** Questions To Consider***

❖ Write about a time in your life where something happened so tragic it stopped you in your tracks.

❖ Were you able to overcome this event? If so, how did you do it and could you apply some of the same methods again if need be?

❖ If you are currently stuck in a rut of life what methods can you use in order to get back on track to victory?

❖ Do you have a support team in place in times of need and if you do can you list 5 of them here?

❖ If you do NOT have a support system in place, how can you go about finding the proper people to put in place? Life events WILL happen. It is a part of the journey and you are better off preparing for the difficult days than not having these things in place at all.

Chapter 11
Mind, Body, And Soul

In the middle of the hustle and bustle of life, it is easy to forget about yourself, especially if you work in an area that is of service to others. You tend to put yourself on the back burner to sacrifice for others. Conversely, this is one of the most dangerous things you can do. I would encourage you to maintain a wellness program you can implement weekly, as this will help you relieve your stress from life by keeping your body healthy as well as helping you to have more energy to put into your KICK in life. This is one of the most important lessons from adding in rest and health wellness to your plan. You want to have the ability to go hard as possible on the days you work but remembering more is not always more. Do not skip meals, stay up later to work, work seven days a week for months at a time or try to LIVE on overtime. You may have times in life when you must push your physical limits to get things done. You cannot realistically expect to work night and day seven days a week forever, without some type of side effect to your body or your quality of work. Trust me, we ALL think we can stay up later than anyone else, take on more of a work load than anyone else. It is not worth it and you are better off working smarter than harder. Protect your body, emotions and mentality so you can have the longevity to do your KICK for the rest of your life. That is more effective than the person that crashes and burns in five years.

Embrace Your Higher Power

Of course I could not close the chapter on Self-care and rejuvenation without speaking to the power of tapping into your higher self. The road to Self-Mastery is a long hard journey not for the faint of heart and you will be lonely at times. You will feel misunderstood by most of the people around because they cannot understand your motivation and drive. They are not meant to understand it because this is **YOUR KICK** not theirs. This does not mean that it will not be emotionally and spiritually draining if you let it. You will need to carve out time to do what it is you need in order to reconnect with the greatest force thereby recharging yourself. Pray, fast, meditate, burn candles, rub oil, whatever it is that you subscribe to, just be sure that you tap into it often. There will be times when you feel as if all the food in the world still leaves you empty, all the coffee and red bull you try to drink will not give you a lift. You will take the proper time to sleep for days and still feel worn out. All you will have is your higher power to utilize and make it through to the other side. I have had many times along my life where I know for a fact I asked myself how in the world did I get past this moment because I know I did not have anything left in the tank.

Rest Your Legs

I mentioned earlier in this publication my time as a Cross Fit Athlete and bodybuilder; along with that lifestyle came more hours than I would care to count in the gym. Days, nights, weekends, holidays etc., if I had a pocket of empty time, I wanted to spend it pounding away at my body. In the beginning, you are proud to be able to make it into the gym three days a week, after some time goes by, you become so engulfed in the culture it becomes a badge of honor to train when you are sick, your birthday, even if there is a hurricane outside. The advanced class to fitness is learning more is not more at all. It took me a long time to learn how valuable rest was for my muscles and nervous system to recharge so that I would be able to go harder my next time in the gym. I had to learn the importance of proper sleep, the benefits this would yield to various parts of my life outside of training. I also had to learn how to take some days in the week to not lift a weight at all, but go to a park take my shoes off in the grass doing natural movements stretching my body, releasing my muscles. At the same time have me out in nature, feet in the dirt and getting actual sunlight on my skin. Pictures on Facebook and Instagram are about who is lifting the most weight, running the fastest, but rarely do you see post about relaxation, mediation, massage, chiropractor visits, acupuncture, hot tubs, etc. These are called the Water Side of training, or the Soft Arts. The heavy lifting, high intensity, more taxing training is referred to as the Fire Side of training, or the Hard Arts.

In this fast pace and hard charged world, we condition ourselves to think harder, but rarely do we take the proper time out to rest and recharge ourselves.

I work in the Mental Health field and one of the main things I see in this culture is that most of us work multiple jobs, travel tons per week driving to our client's homes, have loads of documentation per week with serious deadlines to meet. We feel as if we cannot take our hands off the steering wheel of life for a day because we feel as if the world will fall off its axis if we are not always ON! We must all learn the concept of self -care and how important it is to avoid burnout by running yourself into the ground early. If you cannot utilize your KICK in the world because your body has shut down on you, what good are you or your gifts?

For the go-getters, we are all pretty good at setting up our meetings and appointments for work reasons, I would say that we must be as proactive to pencil in time for days off the grind. Trust me, if you do not make this move you will end up working most of the year and before you realize it, you have not had any time with your loved ones, nor any time doing what it is that gives you life. "All work and no play makes"… you know the rest. I encourage you to take some half days here and there to enjoy doing absolutely nothing. You do not have to spend a ton of money to enjoy yourself and if you like coffee or tea, just sit by a body of water if you have access to it enjoying the sounds of nature. Unplug from all of the phone calls and emails for a while by taking a day to visit your favorite stores, even if you do not buy anything, it can be refreshing being in certain environments you have not seen in months.

Eat To Your KICK!

"What in the world is eating to your Kick Sean?" You must be asking this to yourself, as there is no one set way to eat. Even as a trainer, I never once told a client he or she could ONLY eat this certain way. I will say different lifestyles will require a different demand on the body, and depending on what your KICK is and how much it taxes your body, you should adjust your eating habits to accommodate. Some people such as myself will work at night more than in the day, thus I must be mindful of my water intake during my work shifts because I am not out in the daytime. I must almost force myself to drink more water than usual at night. I travel a lot, so if I must eat out I try to scout some of the best places to go in the cities that I work in or I try to make the best choices possible at the places that I frequent. Once again, no matter how busy I am, not eating is never an option. At the time when fitness and being strong as possible was my focus, I had to force myself to eat way more than usual to fuel my body to lift the entire building every workout. You must have the ability to be aware of your body and your situation to realize that you need to make some adjustments to perform at the highest level within your craft. NFL players, NBA players, boxers, swimmers, business owners, writers, doctors, all have different demands and lifestyles. You cannot expect to be within the field and not make the changes, but still expect to be amongst the best. My favorite quarterback of this day is Tom Brady who is forty years old. On any given Sunday at some point in the game the commentators will speak on the serious diet and training that Brady is known for that gives him an edge on his competition therefore predicting to play more years in the NFL.

On the space provided below and based on what you have read so far, what are some of the things you feel that held you back from achieving your personal level of success?

Chapter 12
The Call To Action!!!

At this point in the process I have given you my life story front to back. I have also provided tools, tricks, tips and methods that helped me achieve the various levels of success I have been blessed to reach up to this very moment. Now it is time for YOU to show and prove who YOU are to yourself! It is time for you to put the book down to go all out executing the specific KICK that YOU declared in the beginning of this book. If you followed the directions, you wrote it down in black and white. I did not give it to you nor did your parents select your KICK, your teachers did not pass it to you; YOU chose it yourself and now it is time to HONOR YOUR WORD! I challenge you to make the necessary phone calls it takes to jump-start your new life. I dare you to send the emails to the proper channels you KNOW could lead you down the path of the new version of yourself. This is a call to action!!! I do not want you to sit the book down and think to yourself, "Man, Sean said some cool things in this book." I want you to go out with fire under your feet, courage in your heart as you tackle your particular selected craft. I want you to take massive action right away even if it is not a long drawn out thought process. I do not care if it seems far-fetched, it does not matter if it does not work. There is magic to be unlocked with the process of having a thought in your mind and working very hard towards it. The process is bound to bring something into your life that will make the journey well worth it. Even if the end result is not exactly the way you pictured it, you will be further along than where you are at this moment.

My next challenge to you is to find a mentor that will drive you and push you towards your goals, not someone who will pat you on the back when you fall short telling you it will be alright. Find someone that will step on your toes and make you so uncomfortable, you feel like all there is for you is success. Facing this person again after coming up short is not an option, and it will not be an easy pill to swallow. It will totally go against your natural inclination for gratification, but that is why it is called a challenge right? If it does not challenge you it will not change you!

My final challenge I will issue is to do something that will help someone else which has absolutely nothing to do with satisfying you. Go out into the world and help someone to be the best version of themselves even in the smallest form possible. How grand of a sacrifice you make is not the point and it does not take a lot of change to shift someone's paradigm. Mostly, people simply need to know that a person out there actually cares about their wellbeing. Finding your KICK makes your life worth living, but the ultimate fact is that your KICK was a gift from the creator, as it was never meant for you to harbor it for yourself. You are supposed to use your gifts, talents, and wisdom to be a example for the world. Trust me, it can be lonely at the top and only a select few will stay be by your side when the smoke clears and the lights go off. By making a real impact in people's life you will make true connections that can last a lifetime. This leads us to my next work…

"The Power Of Your Circle"

Coming in 2018'

Points To Consider

❖ When was the last time you had a vacation of 4 days or more?

❖ What can you adjust in your day-to-day life to give yourself some breathing room from the grind?

❖ Do you take out time to practice your spiritual practices?

❖ What is your favorite place to be and when is the last time you were there?

❖ Before you got a family and the busy lifestyle would do you love to do with your free time? When is the last time you've done it?

❖ When was the last time you used your Personal Time Off?

❖ What is it that you cannot wait to get off to do?

Recommended Reading:

Mastery by: Robert Greene

The 50th Law by: Robert Greene

Strength Finder 2.0 by: Tom Rath

Living the 7 Habits by: Steve Covey

Act Like A Success, Think Like A Success by: Steve Harvey

King by: Elliot Husle

Accelerated Learning by: Brian Tracy

Greatness Is Upon You by: Eric Thomas

Average Skills, Phenomenal Will by: Eric Thomas

Secret To Success by: Eric Thomas

The Laws Of Success by: Napoleon Hill

The Art Of Learning by: Josh Waitzken

Unlimited Power by: Tony Robbins

As A Man Thinketh by: James Allen

Your Mind And How To Use It by: William Atkinson

The Art Of Mental Training by: D. C. Gonzalez

The School Of Greatness by: Lewis Howes

The Power Of Concentration by: Theron Q. Dumont

Awaken The Giant Within by: Tony Robbins

Think And Grow Rich, A Black Choice by Dennis Kimbro

What Makes The Great, Great by: Dennis Kimbro

Relentless by: Tim Grove

Outliers by: Malcom Gladwell

Double Your Productivity by Brian Tracy

The Power Of Self-Discipline by: Brian Tracy

Goals! by: Brian Tracy

48 Laws Of Power by: Robert Greene

The 4-Hour Work Week by: Tim Ferris

Biography

Seanathan Polidore, born and raised in Franklin Louisiana, currently residing in St. Martinville Louisiana with his wife Tallya Polidore and their three children. He acquired his Master's Degree in Psychology from the University Of Phoenix and is currently pursuing his Doctoral Degree in Psychology. Mr. Polidore is employed as a Child Psychologist servicing the Acadiana Region, he is also a Motivational Speaker with the Personal Empowerment Network, an on air radio personality, and an author. His one mission in life is to "Empower and Enlighten" as many people as to have them DO FOR SELF, have them realize their own power to do and be what they desire with emphasis on "Doing The Work!"

What's Your KICK?

The Guide To Unlocking Your Passion

By: Seanathan Polidore

Editor: Anthony G. Bell, Jr.

Artwork By: Antoine "Ghost" Mitchell

Copyright © 2017 By: Seanathan Polidore

Library Of Congress Cataloging-In-Publication Data available upon request.

ISBN: 978-0-692-99177-0

What's Your KICK?

The Guide To Unlocking Your Passion

I wish I had this book 10 years ago. Sean has definitely kicked himself into a well-deserved position amongst the best "self-help" books. The book does not come off as preachy as if he knows the way everything should go, but more of a conversation that you should have with someone that wants the best for you. ~ Bethany Denise

After reading the book, not only did I confirm what my kick was, I was given more clarity on how to go about achieving what I felt was placed in me to accomplish. This book gives strategies and a clear method on how to go about doing it. From minimizing distractions to getting a mentor, it gives a clear path forward on what steps to take.

Mr. Polidore's method of disseminating the information, as well as his transparency in sharing his own experiences, make for a great read that is not only impactful, but also relatable. His passion comes through in the words he has written, which I found very motivating as a reader! I found it to be much more than just a book, but a loud, clear call to action! ~ Corey Jack – Entrepreneur

$20.00
ISBN 978-0-692-99177-0
52000>

9 780692 991770

Made in the USA
Middletown, DE
07 December 2018